T5-CNZ-850

J266.092   00003504
BUT   Butler, Mary and Trent
          The John Allen Moores: good news in war and peace

The John Allen Moores: Good news in war and peace.

DATE DUE

VBS-91			
JY 24 '94			

FIRST BAPTIST CHURCH
LIBRARY
TOMBALL, TEXAS

The John Allen Moores:
Good News in War and Peace

MARY AND TRENT BUTLER
Illustrated by Dick Wahl

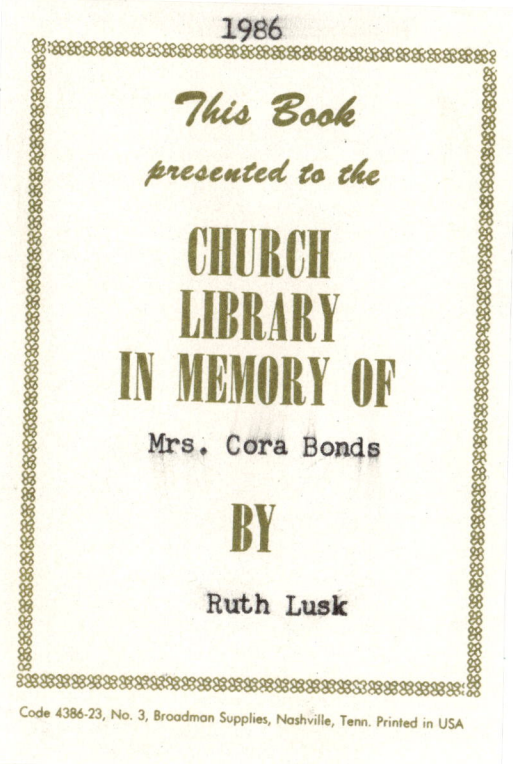

1986

This Book presented to the

CHURCH LIBRARY IN MEMORY OF

Mrs. Cora Bonds

BY

Ruth Lusk

Code 4386-23, No. 3, Broadman Supplies, Nashville, Tenn. Printed in USA

BROADMAN PRESS
Nashville, Tennessee

FIRST BAPTIST CHURCH LIBRARY
TOMBALL, TEXAS

Dedicated to the memory
of Mr. and Mrs. Sibley Burnett
who by example and teaching
inspired us to be missionaries;
and to Curt and Kevin,
who were very special MK's.

© Copyright 1985 • Broadman Press
All Rights Reserved
4242-95
ISBN: 0-8054-4295-2
Dewey Decimal Classification: J266.092
Subject Headings:
MOORE, JOHN ALLEN // MOORE, PAULINE // MISSIONS—EUROPE
Library of Congress Catalog Number: 85-6656
Printed in the United States of America

Library of Congress Cataloging in Publication Data

Butler, Mary, 1943–
  The John Allen Moores.

  (Meet the missionary series)
  1. Moore, John Allen—Juvenile literature.
2. Moore, Pauline—Juvenile literature. 3. Missionaries
—Europe—Biography—Juvenile literature.
4. Missionaries—United States—Biography—Juvenile
literature. 5. Missions—Europe—Juvenile literature.
I. Butler, Trent C. II. Wahl, Richard, 1939–
III. Title. IV. Series.
BV2855.6.M66B87 1985   266'.0092'2 [B]   85-6656
ISBN 0-8054-4295-2

Contents

Playing for Keeps 5
Race with Death 8
Pauline: Child of the South 15
What Shall I Do? 19
Working and Waiting 28
The Case of the Chocolate Mashies 34
War 42
Beginning Again 51
Lady Preacher 58
Make Your Own Missionary Adventure 63
Meet the Authors 64

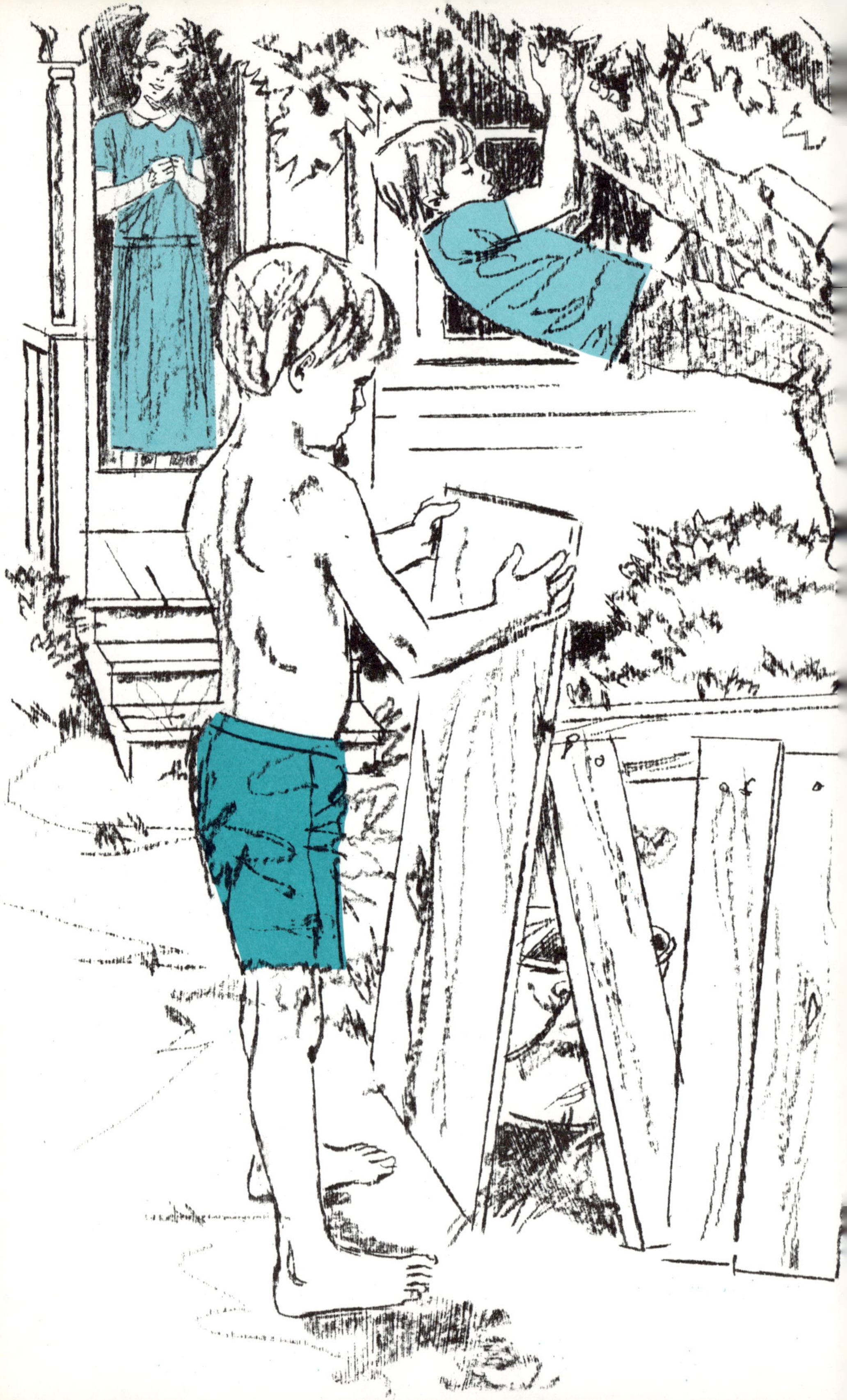

Playing for Keeps

"John Allen! John Allen! Come in here a minute, please!"

Eight-year-old John Allen looked up from the yard. He wiped his dusty, bare feet against the back of his bare legs. "Be back in a minute," he called to his playmate. "Don't tear down my fort. Mother wants me for something."

He ran towards the house. "What could Mother want?" he wondered. He opened the screen door and faced his mother.

"John Allen, have you been shooting marbles with the other boys?"

"No, Ma'am. We have been just playing in the yard." John Allen was relieved it was no worse than that.

"Now, John Allen! You know I did not mean just this minute."

"OK, Mother. I played marbles with the boys yesterday afternoon. Everyone was playing. You don't want me to be the only one left out, do you?"

"John Allen, a neighbor told me today that some of the boys are playing marbles for keeps. What do you know about that?"

John sighed. "Yes, Ma'am. Some of them are. But we didn't yesterday. We were just having fun. And I won."

"Let me tell you what I'll do, John Allen. It's not too long until Christmas. I will give you a nickel each day that you don't play marbles for keeps. How about that? OK?"

John Allen glanced up at his mother. "I'll try," he promised. As he started toward the yard again, he heard a familiar whistle.

"Hey, John Allen! Both of you come play with us," called his best buddy.

"See you, Mother," John Allen called as he and his playmate ran out to join his friends. But John Allen stopped suddenly. The boys were all stooped over in a circle. He knew what was happening.

"Come on, we're just getting started," his friend hollered. A lump rose in John Allen's throat. He saw the marbles spread out in the circle on the sidewalk. He knew what that meant.

The other boys looked up. "Hey, John Allen, you are just in time. We've been practicing. You're not going to beat us today!"

John Allen rubbed his hands together. He remembered the fun he had had yesterday. He could still see his nice red marble knocking all the others out of the circle. But he could also hear his mother's voice. His mother might even be looking out the front window now. Finally, he walked to the circle.

"Well, I can play with you. But we can't play for keeps," he told them. The other boys laughed. But John Allen stood firm. He allowed no more playing for keeps when he was in the game. He knew just what he wanted to do with those nickels.

During the next few days he began counting the nickels he was to get. On the next Saturday he came in from play early. He washed his hands and wandered into the kitchen. His mother stood over a big pot that was boiling on the stove. "What are you doing in so early?" she asked.

"I thought maybe you would give me my nickels. I haven't played marbles for keeps. I want to run down to the store before it closes."

Soon John Allen was running swiftly down the street,

clutching his nickels tightly. He would buy "jawbreakers," licorice strips, and maybe an almond-chocolate bar or two!

John Allen liked his hometown of Tupelo, Mississippi. He had moved there with his family when he was eight-and-a-half years old. He knew most of the people in the town. His father, William, was a salesman for a shoe company. Mr. Moore traveled from one town to another in a Model T Ford car. He would take the backseat out and load the car with long, flat cases of shoes. He did not take pairs of shoes, just one shoe of each kind. He would show these to the merchants. They would select the ones they liked. Mr. Moore would make a list of his orders and send it to his boss in the big city. His boss would then send the shoes in large boxes to the stores.

William Moore was known by the storekeepers throughout northern Mississippi. At first he sold only shoes. A few years later he sold cloth for the women to make clothes. Still later, he sold insurance. His selling jobs kept him out of town a lot. John Allen always looked forward to Friday night when his father would return home.

During the week, John Allen enjoyed talking with his mother. She was well-educated. She told John Allen many interesting things. One night after his mother told the children good night, John Allen heard her praying.

"Dear Lord," she said, "I thank You for our children—for Virgil, for Merrill, for Frances, and for John Allen. Help them to grow up to be good people. Let them serve You well in whatever way You want them to. Amen."

Race with Death

"Come on, John Allen," Mother called. "Time to get up and go to church."

"Be there in a minute. You know I don't want to miss Sunday School. What would Mr. Leake say?"

John Allen liked to go to Sunday School with his mother. Sometimes he asked why his father always went to the First Christian Church. "That's where he's always gone," Mother would explain.

This Sunday morning John Allen was really excited. The Junior Department had something special planned. Last Sunday Mr. M. E. Leake, the department superintendent, had promised the boys and girls a surprise. John Allen liked the surprises the fat, jolly man had for them. John Allen knew how much Mr. Leake hoped each boy and girl would become a Christian before they were promoted out of the Junior Department.

John Allen hurried to his Sunday School department. Sure enough, Mr. Leake had a surprise. The pastor was going to speak just to the Juniors before they went to their classes. When he finished, the pastor asked how many would like to become Christians. John Allen joined several of his friends. They went up and shook hands with the pastor and Mr. Leake. John Allen told the pastor he would like to be a Christian.

All the boys were extra fidgety during the Sunday School class period. One boy leaned over to John Allen. "I have become a Christian and I'm going to join the church today," he exclaimed. "Why don't you?"

After Sunday School was over, John Allen ran to his mother in the church auditorium. "My friend is going to join the church this morning. Can I join?"

"I'm so happy you want to do this, John Allen," his mother said. "But this is a very important decision. Please wait until we can talk about it. Then, after you are sure you have become a Christian, you can join."

"When can we talk about it?" John Allen asked.

"When we get home from church."

As Mrs. Moore prepared the noon meal, John Allen walked around the house impatiently. "How long will it be before we can talk?" he asked.

"Right after we eat," his mother assured him. John Allen thought the time would never come. He wanted to get the thing settled. He knew what he should do, and he wanted to do it.

Finally the time came. Mrs. Moore asked several questions. John Allen showed he understood about sin and his need for Jesus Christ to forgive his sins.

"Have you told Jesus about your sins, John Allen, and asked Him to forgive you"

"Yes, Ma'am. I did that this morning in Sunday School."

"Have you asked Jesus to come into your life?"

"I sure have, Mother."

"I think you understand what you are saying, John Allen. Do you know who is preaching at our church next Sunday?"

"Brother Dickinson, I guess," replied John Allen.

"No. Merrill is going to preach. He has decided God wants him to be a preacher. He'll be coming home from college this week. He has finished his first year at Mississippi College."

The next Sunday John Allen could hardly wait for his brother, Merrill, to quit preaching. John Allen went down

9

as soon as the singing began. He was anxious to tell people that he had become a Christian. A few Sundays later he was baptized.

Bang went the door as John Allen ran and skipped out into the yard. He looked up and down the street. Soon his father would be back from his weekly selling rounds. Each Friday John Allen helped his father carry the sample shoes into the house. John Allen liked to look through the shoes and dream about the time when he could wear such fine things.

John Allen heard the Model T. He heard it rattling before he saw his father turning into the driveway. Father always let John Allen drive around the block. Sometimes Frances, who was six years younger, climbed in with him.

John Allen greeted his father. He always wanted to tell him everything that had happened during the week.

"Papa, Papa, let's go downtown." Then John Allen stole a

quick look into his father's eyes. He knew Papa was tired from the long week. Still John Allen wanted the adventure of driving downtown. "Can we go, Papa? Can we?"

"OK, Son. Just a minute. Let me have a word with your mother. Get in the car."

John Allen jumped in behind the big steering wheel. He put his hands on the wheel and imagined he was racing down the highway. He turned the wheel this way and that to make the big curves. He pulled at the brake to avoid a big dog racing across the street. Just then Papa slipped in beside him.

"Here are the keys, John Allen. You ready for the big downtown trip?"

John Allen came back to the real world. "Sure, Papa. Let's go. What's the first stop?"

John Allen drove slowly to the center of the small town. "Park there in front of the drugstore," Mr. Moore said. John Allen carefully parked the car against the curb, just as his father had taught him. He turned the car off and took the keys out. His father always taught him to protect the car from thieves. Then he looked up—into the eyes of the city policeman!

"Hi, John Allen. How are you, Mr. Moore? What's going on here?"

John Allen looked down at his bare feet. "Oh no, what is going to happen now," he thought. "Will I ever get to drive again? Surely he won't give me a ticket. We don't have any money to pay a fine."

"Mr. Moore," the policeman said. "Isn't John Allen a little young to be driving?" Of course, the policeman didn't mention a driver's license. They were not in use at that time.

Papa Moore scratched his head. "Yes, sir," he nodded. "He is a mite young, but he is a mighty good driver. After I have been on the road all week, I like to let him take over."

The policeman took off his cap. John Allen could see the

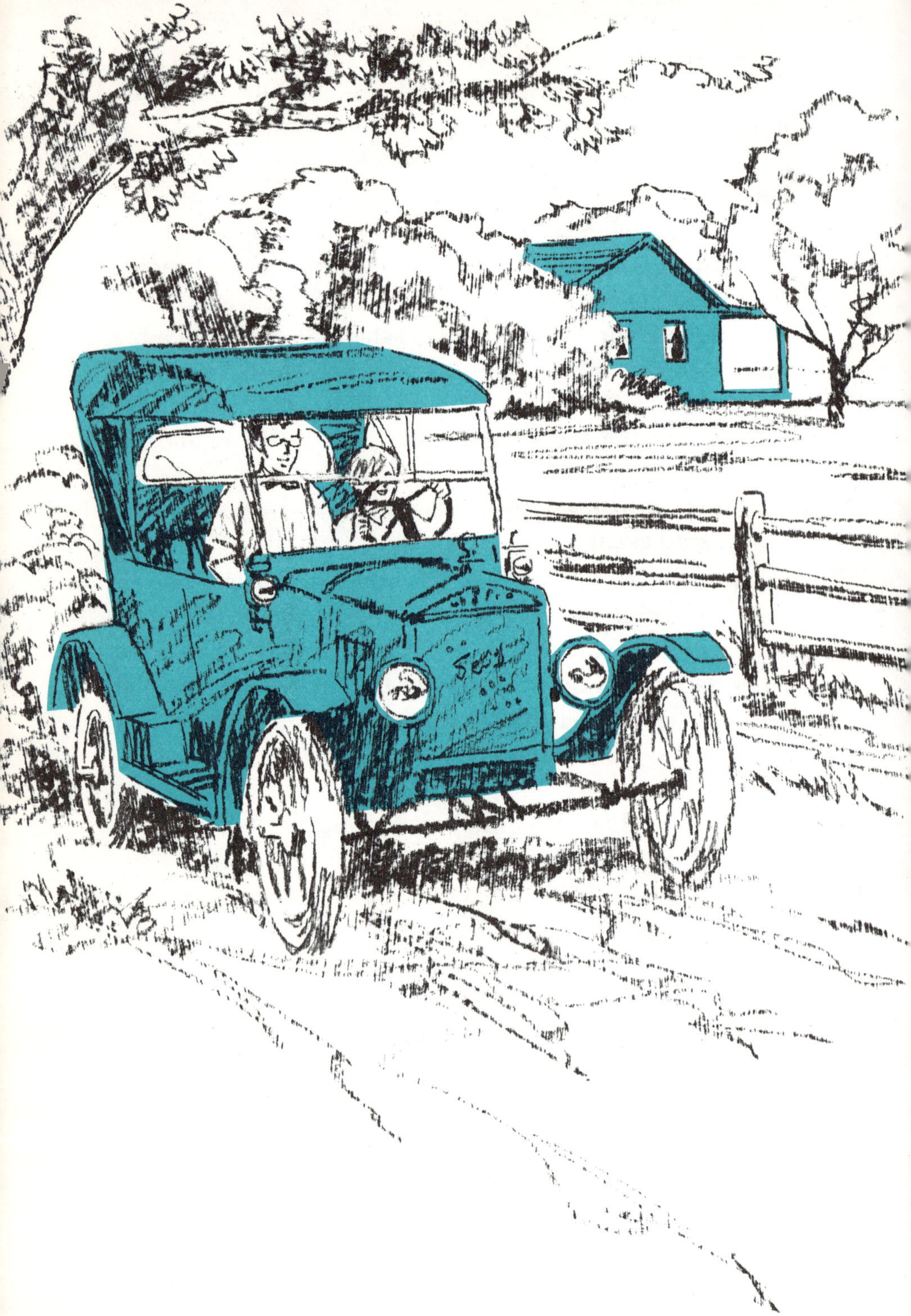

question mark in his face. Finally, he placed the cap back on his head. His face broke into a smile. "All right, but be careful," he said and walked on down the street.

John Allen followed his papa into the general store. "Bit late with the newspaper, aren't you, John Allen," the owner greeted him with a grin.

"You got your paper hours ago," John Allen replied. "You don't get another one until Tuesday." John Allen enjoyed kidding with the friendly store owner. He also enjoyed his job delivering the *Tupelo Journal*. Each Tuesday and Friday he picked up his seventy papers from Mr. Kincannon, the owner and editor. John Allen would fold the papers. A big edition of more than eight pages made his work a lot harder. He had to slip one section into the other before folding. Then John Allen would walk or ride his bicycle to his seventy customers.

Sometimes he got a chance to make extra money. One of the merchants might publish a special advertising circular. John Allen would deliver them all over Tupelo. Then he would ride proudly home, run up to his mother, and say, "Look, Mother. I got an extra seventy-five cents today."

"How'd you do that?" Mrs. Moore would ask with a smile.

"Delivered circulars all over town again. Just look at these clothing sales." Mother would come to look. Together they would dream of buying all the pretty things in the circular.

Sometimes, after his hard work, John Allen would decide he had earned a special treat. He would ride his bike out to the water tank. He would climb carefully up onto the tank. He could see almost all of Tupelo and the countryside beyond. These were some of his favorite moments. He also took time to sit and think about the future. He often tried to picture a big university city where he might go to college. But that was hard to do because he had been out of Tupelo so seldom.

John Allen found many ways to fulfill his yearning to climb. Sometimes he just went down to the courthouse. He would climb up the old stairs to the clock tower. The tower was nearly as high as the water tank. From there, he could see nearly everything in Tupelo.

After one of his climbing adventures, John Allen came home chuckling to himself. He stopped in mid-chuckle when he saw his mother's worried face. "What's wrong?" John Allen asked. He had never seen his mother quite like this.

"We got a phone call that Pa is very ill," she answered. (Pa was the name they used for John Allen's grandfather.) "When your father and Virgil get home, they'll have to drive down there in a hurry. It may be too late already."

John Allen sat quietly in the corner of the sofa and listened. "Wish I could go, too," he whispered to himself. He walked outside with the others to wait.

Soon Papa drove up. His mother told him the news. Quickly they got everything ready for him and Virgil to go. Papa looked down at John Allen. "Take good care of Mother and Frances, John Allen. We will come back just as soon as we can."

The travelers returned a few days later. They looked tired and sad. John Allen ran to his father and threw his arms around his waist. "How did the trip go, Papa?"

"It was hard, John Allen. Pa died. We just made it. Had an awful time. Maybe Virgil had better tell you about it."

"Papa really wanted to get there. He pushed that old Model T about as hard as she would go. Little too hard, I guess. I looked down to see why my legs were feeling so warm. 'Papa,' I screamed, 'the floorboard's on fire.' Papa stopped that car right on a dime. We leaped out and started pulling those floor boards right out of the car. We left them by the side of the road and raced on our way. We got there just in time to say good-bye to Pa."

"What a story!" John Allen muttered to himself. "I ought to write that up for the *Tupelo Journal*."

John Allen went up to his room to write his first story, "A Race with Death." He made several attempts but never did finish it. Still, John Allen decided right then that he wanted to write stories when he grew up!

Pauline: Child of the South

In another city, many miles from Tupelo, Pauline Willingham was growing up. She liked to sit in the big auditorium and look at the stained glass windows in the First Baptist Church of Macon, Georgia. She felt like it was "her" church. She was proud to be part of it. Her daddy had been the second person baptized in this church. Her church had sent out the first Southern Baptist as a doctor missionary to China.

On this particular day, Pauline was remembering. She closed her eyes and tried to imagine the early days of Macon. The little town on the river had grown. It was a city now.

Pauline opened her eyes. Yes, this was "her" church. She closed her eyes tight once more and thought back to a morning when she was nine years old. She had gone into her parents' room. "Mother, Daddy, can I get in bed with you? It is so cold in my room."

Her mother smiled sleepily. "Yes, Pauline. Come, get in here under our feather quilt. We have a little while before it is time to get ready for church."

Pauline snuggled in under the covers with them. How

15

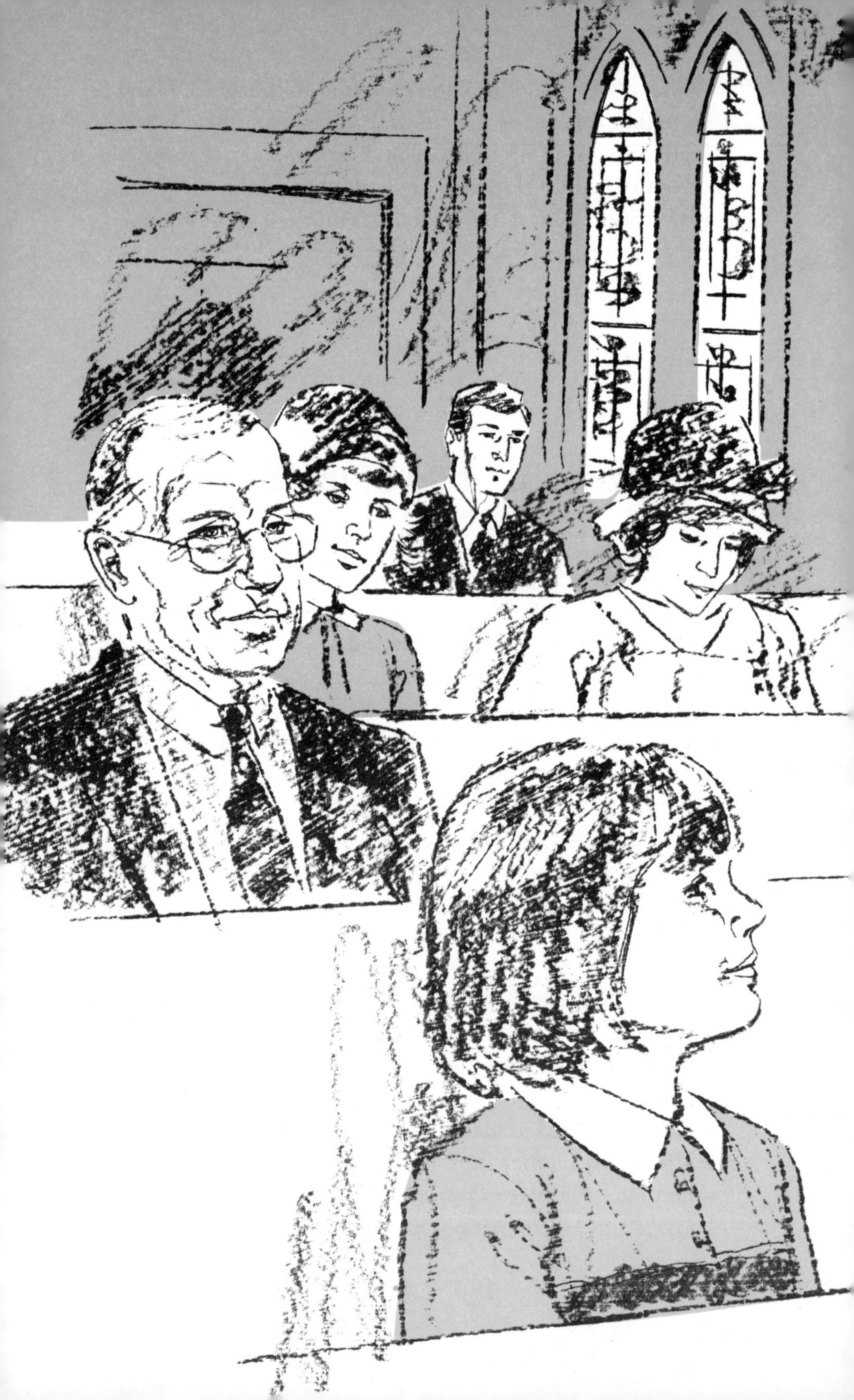

she liked that! She felt warm and secure. Love surrounded her there. "Mother, do you know what I have been thinking about?"

"What, Pauline?" her mother asked gently.

"Yes, tell us," her father nodded.

"I want you to tell me how to become a Christian. I think I am ready to do that."

Now, Pauline could still feel the warmth and excitement that she had felt when her mother had told her how Jesus loved her. "I am only nine," Pauline remembered saying. "Some people say this is too young. But I know what I want to do."

Again Pauline opened her eyes and watched the sunshine dance through the colored windows of the church. She remembered stepping into the aisle of "her" church. "I love Jesus," she had said to herself as she walked down to tell the pastor. She had given her life to Jesus that day. It was one of the happiest days of her life.

Pauline remembered then about the day her family moved. This was another happy day for Pauline. She couldn't wait to be in their new house. Her mother called their old house a funny name—the Rat's Nest. Still Pauline remembered liking that old house. She had so many favorite places to run and hide in. She would never forget the happy memories of the Rat's Nest.

"Hurry up, Pauline," her sister Sarah called. "We must go to school this morning before we go to the new house."

Pauline stamped her foot in a huff. She wanted one last look at their old Rat's Nest. She did not want to forget anything about it.

Finally she turned to pick up her books. Then off they went. Pauline did not learn much at school that day. She kept thinking of the new house. At last, the bell rang. She rushed out and turned in a new direction from school. She hurried to her new home, to her very own room. Here she knew she would have many things to remember.

Again, Pauline remembered as she sat in "her" church. She thought of the day when she had raced out the front door of the new house. "Here's the bus," she yelled to her sister. "We're going to miss it." Pauline saw Sarah and her mother laughing as they ran to catch the bus. This was their happy shopping day together. The kind bus driver saw them coming and waited.

"Let's sit here close to the door," Sarah puffed to her Mother.

"Oh, yes," echoed Pauline. "Here are some seats." Mother nodded to the children as they bounded into the empty seats.

Suddenly, the bus jerked to a halt. Pauline stuck her head out the window. She wanted to see what was happening. An elderly man waited for the bus. He trembled as he reached for the first step on the bus. With a thud, his walking cane missed the step and slipped from his hand to the street. He bent down to find the cane.

"Oh, Mother," Pauline shouted. "Do you see that man? He's real old and feeble. He wants to get on the bus, but he cannot make it."

Mrs. Willingham did not answer. She was already in action. She stepped down into the street. Reaching under the bus, she picked up the cane. A smile lighted the old face as the man took back his cane. Again he attempted the climb into the bus. This time with Mrs. Willingham at his elbow, he made it. She guided him into an empty seat.

"Oh, Sarah," sighed Pauline. "Isn't Mother wonderful. She loves everybody. And she helps everybody she meets."

Pauline kept sitting in the pew at "her" church. She thought back to her Primary days in Sunday School, when she was only seven years old. The church had an evening for the family. Everyone came to church to have fun together.

Mother had prepared a skit based on the story of the "Old Woman Who Lived in the Shoe." The skit provided parts for all the children in her Primary Department in Sunday School. To start the skit, the children rolled out a huge shoe. A carpenter had made it for the children to ride in. Several children peeked out of the shoe. Others walked beside it. Mother came out on stage without her false teeth. Everyone in the church screamed and hollered. She was such a sight. But one person did not join the laughter. Daddy could hardly believe what he was seeing. He did not think it was funny.

Pauline decided right then she would always try to have a good time and to help others have a good time.

What Shall I Do?

Back in Tupelo, John Allen's chance finally came. He had saved money from all his jobs. Still he had very little. And it was time to go to college. How could he get enough money? His parents certainly did not have enough money to help him.

His aunt Selma Maxville had said she would help. Aunt Selma was a missionary to Burma. John was grateful for her check. But it was still not enough.

Finally a letter came. It offered a small scholarship to Mississippi College. That would help, but it was not much. The college was over two hundred miles from Tupelo. But it was a Baptist college. Merrill had gone there. Some of John Allen's friends from Tupelo were there. He wanted to go, but how could he afford it?

Other letters made the decision harder. Emory University in Atlanta, Georgia, heard that John Allen had written for his high school paper. They offered him a big scholarship to study journalism. "But," reasoned John Allen, "Emory is not a Baptist college. I have always wanted to go to a Baptist college."

John Allen had another choice. Howard College in Alabama (now Samford University) was a Baptist school. He had heard about a scholarship, slightly larger, offered to students who planned to be preachers. Howard College was a lot closer to Tupelo.

John Allen had to be honest. He did not know what he wanted to be or do. However, one day in church he had gone forward during the final invitation hymn. He told the preacher he felt God wanted him in full-time church work of some sort.

John Allen sat at the table at home with the college papers spread out before him. "What shall I do?" he asked himself. "I might become a preacher. Then again, I might not. If I don't, it wouldn't be right to take the scholarship to Howard. I'll go to Mississippi College."

At college John Allen faced another tough decision. He seemed to be almost the only boy with a double name. "I will just introduce myself to everybody as John at college," he decided. "When I go back to Tupelo, everyone will still call me John Allen anyway." From that time, John Allen was John to some people and John Allen to others.

The first semester at college was hard. He could not find a job. He very carefully used the money his aunt had given him. The second semester he got a job in the college dining hall waiting tables. For this work he got his meals free.

One day John Allen ran to the dining hall to work. He was worried because he was a few minutes late. He hung

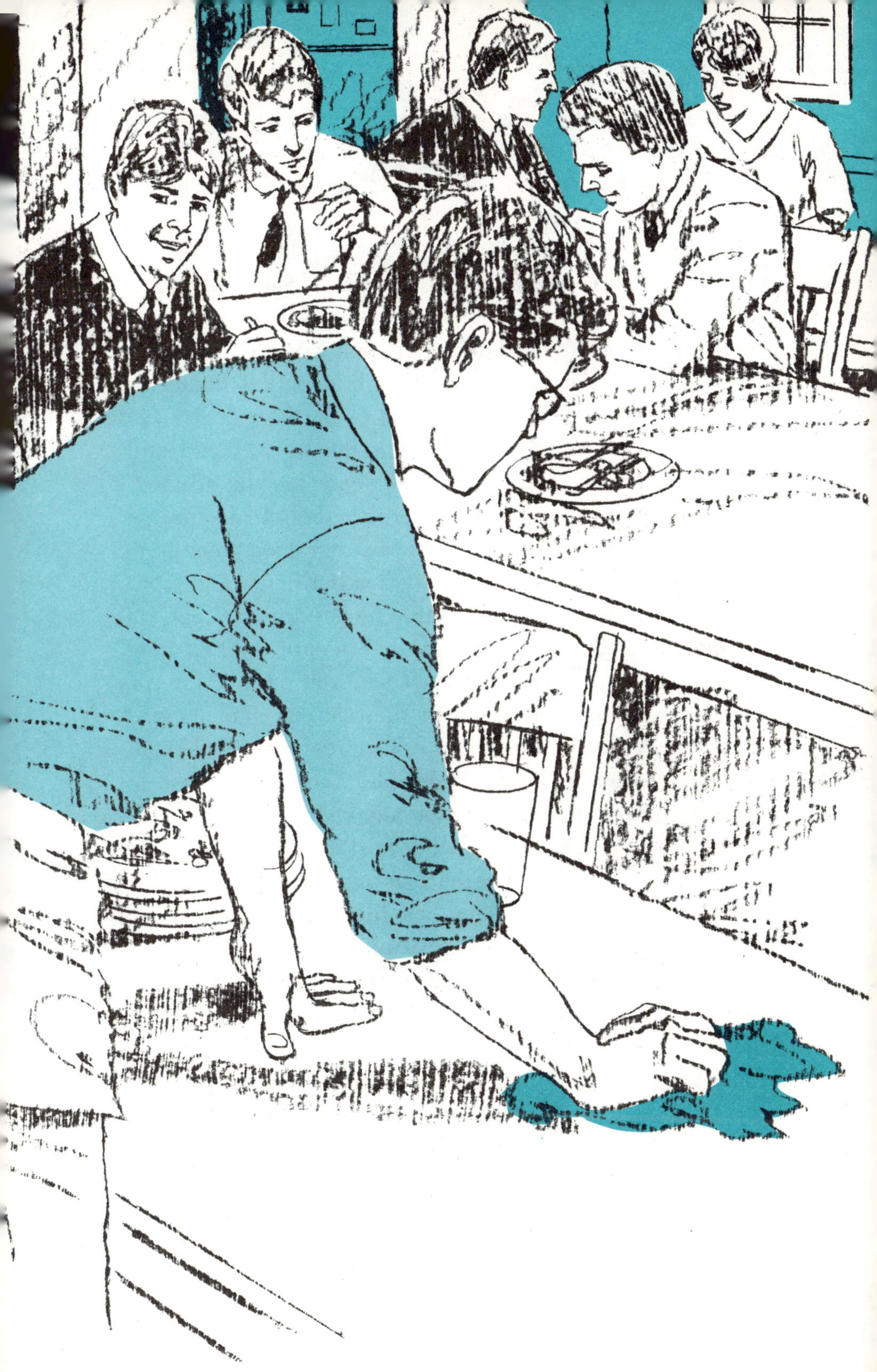

up his dripping raincoat. Then he began setting the tables. Suddenly the door swung open. His friend rushed through. John Allen looked up quickly. Then he looked again.

"What is that around your waist?" he asked in amazement.

"Oh nothing," came the reply. "Just a pillow for the belt line." The friend lifted a finger to his lips. "Shh! Don't tell."

"One good thing about working in the dining hall," John Allen said, "I don't have to run the belt line anymore. The upperclassmen don't keep the belt line until I finish my work!"

John Allen rubbed his hand on his hip. "I can still almost feel the sore spots from last semester." he grinned. He would never forget that first rainy day at Mississippi College. He had noticed all the upperclassmen come in to the dining hall wearing long, wide leather belts.

"We just want to welcome you to Mississippi College," a sophomore laughingly said. That had meant the belt line! On rainy evenings, the upperclassmen would line up in two rows. They held their belts in their hands and slapped them eagerly against their thighs. The freshmen would stall over their plates as long as possible. Finally they had to leave the dining hall. There was only one door.

The freshmen ran as fast and hard as they could. The upperclassmen swung the belts as hard and fast as they could as the freshmen rushed past them to the door.

"Get to work, Freshman!" the dining hall boss called.

John Allen jumped and went back to setting tables. He looked up with a brief prayer of thanks. "I sure am glad I have to work," he thought. "Maybe being poor has its good side after all."

John worked hard all through college. He was janitor of the Baptist church. Then he was manager of a dormitory where students lived. During his last year he helped a professor in the English department.

John Allen also studied hard. By his second year he had decided to become a preacher. Merrill, his brother, was a pastor in Selma, Alabama. He asked John Allen to come and preach his first sermon in his church. That was exciting. He preached quite a lot after that. One summer he preached for youth revivals in eight churches. His last year in college his church had a special service. They ordained John Allen to be a preacher. Merrill preached the sermon for his ordination.

Later, Merrill went to see John Allen at college. The two brothers walked around the college campus. "Merrill, I probably will not be a pastor in this country long. I really think I want to serve God some other way. Maybe in another country. I am not really sure just what I'll do or where I'll go."

Merrill looked at John Allen and gave him a friendly pat on the shoulder. "Don't worry. Do what you know is right at this time. God will show you what to do a little at a time."

God soon showed John Allen the next step. John Allen knew he needed more schooling to be a preacher. The place he had in mind was in Louisville, Kentucky. It was called The Southern Baptist Theological Seminary. Merrill had gone there. John Allen wanted to go, too.

"I don't guess I can go anytime soon, though," John Allen thought. "There's no one to help me. I have no money. The semester has already begun. I just do not know what God wants me to do now."

John Allen was living in Tupelo again, waiting to see what he could do. He was standing in the bank one day, when he saw an old friend. "Mr. Leake, so good to see you. It has been a long time since you helped me know Jesus back in the Junior Department."

"Hi, John Allen. Glad I ran into you. I have something I have been meaning to give to you." He handed John Allen a check for ten dollars.

"Thank you, Mr. Leake. God has just used you again at an important moment in my life. I'll use this to buy a ticket on the train to Louisville. Then I can go to the seminary."

John Allen bought the ticket and even paid some money that he owed with the ten dollars. He arrived in Louisville a week after classes had started. He had exactly $1.49 in his pocket. He quickly looked up Leo Green, his school friend from Tupelo and Mississippi College. Leo loaned him the books he needed for his classes. He also helped him find jobs to make money. Another friend from Mississippi College helped him find a church to pastor. W. O. Vaught was moving away and leaving the church in Salvisa, Kentucky. He told the church John Allen Moore would be a good pastor for them. The church agreed and called John Allen to be their pastor.

John Allen was thrilled. He knew his brother was right. God would lead one step at a time.

John Allen studied hard at the seminary. One day he was walking down the hall thinking to himself. "What should I do when I finish this last year in seminary?" He saw a sign which read: "Dr. Charles Maddry, Foreign Mission Board executive secretary, is on campus to interview students."

"I wonder if that is what God has for me?" John Allen wondered. He thought back to his conversation with Merrill. "I have always known I would not be a pastor here long," he remembered. "I guess God gave me that idea with that book about Solomon Ginsberg, the missionary to Brazil. I was about ten when I read that book."

John Allen felt God wanted him to talk to Dr. Maddry. He walked to Dr. Maddry's door. "What can I do for you?" the distinguished man asked, as John Allen walked in. "Are you thinking about foreign mission work?"

"I have not really had time to think about it lately," he smiled. "Studying, working, and pastoring is enough for me to think about. I used to think about it some." He related his experiences to Dr. Maddry.

"Do you have any reason you could not be a missionary," Dr. Maddry asked in a friendly way.

"Well, maybe one, sir. I have flat feet. Do you think I could be a missionary with flat feet?" He had heard about young men who wanted to become soldiers being turned down for this reason.

Dr. Maddry smiled. "Yes, Mr. Moore, I do believe we might arrange for you to be a missionary somewhere even with flat feet. That is if the Lord leads you in that direction."

"What could I do as a missionary?" John Allen wanted to know.

"You might teach in a seminary or college or work in a number of other areas of service. I do hope you will think about applying. The 1930s have been hard on us. The Foreign Mission Board did not have enough money to send missionaries to other countries. Now, Southern Baptists have made it possible for the Board to send out more missionaries. I look forward to hearing from you."

The meeting with Dr. Maddry set John Allen to thinking and worrying. Should he become a missionary? He knew people who said, "God told me to go to China" Or "God called me to go to Brazil." John Allen thought God had told him to go, but He had not said where.

A few weeks later, John Allen saw an old friend named Lemuel Hall at Louisville. The Halls had been the Moores' neighbors in Tupelo. John Allen had gone to school with two of Lemuel Hall's brothers. Now Pastor Lemuel Hall was the Foreign Mission Board member from Illinois. He was in Louisville for a meeting and John Allen invited him to come to his dormitory.

"Brother Hall, I have a problem."

"What is it, John Allen?"

"I have talked with Dr. Maddry and have written to the Foreign Mission Board. They want me to go to their headquarters in Richmond, Virginia. They want to ask me questions and give me some tests. If everything goes well, they want to appoint me as a missionary."

"That sounds wonderful," Mr. Hall interrupted. "I certainly do not see any problem."

"But Brother Hall, I'm a bit worried. God has not led me to any one country. What shall I say when the Foreign Mission Board asks me where I want to go?"

"Don't worry about that, John Allen. We need people to serve in many countries. We will be delighted to receive your application. The Board will send you where the need is greatest."

John Allen was so glad to hear that. He knew God had led him another step along the way.

Later, John Allen went to Richmond and passed all the tests. Again he talked with Dr. Maddry. "I've been thinking a lot about Brazil," John Allen said.

"Fine," said Dr. Maddry. "But we have one small problem. We just sent two couples to Brazil. Let me talk to you about seven other places on this map," he told John, pointing to a world map. "Since you are interested in teaching, why don't we send you to teach in the seminary in Bucharest, Rumania?"

"That's fine with me," John Allen said, as he nodded his enthusiastic agreement.

After graduation, John Allen went back to Tupelo. He realized he knew nothing at all about Rumania. He went to the library and checked out every book he could find about the little country in eastern Europe. One day, as he was reading, his mother brought in the mail. "Here's a letter for you, John Allen. It's from Richmond."

John Allen looked at the envelope. It was from Dr. Maddry. That worried him. "Had something happened? Weren't they going to send him as a missionary?" He ripped open the letter.

"Dear John:

"I enjoyed our visit in Richmond recently. I am so glad God is leading you to be a missionary. In our talk you indicated you wanted to go where the need is the greatest. I have talked with many of the people who help us here in Richmond. They reminded me we have been looking for someone to go to Yugoslavia for sixteen years. We believe you are that person. We are praying that God will lead you to go to Yugoslavia for us. A boat sails in two weeks.

"Sincerely yours,
Charles Maddry"

"What is it, John Allen? What is it?" his mother asked.

"They are sending me to Yugoslavia. I must be ready in two weeks."

"John Allen, I am so proud of you. Thank God for this opportunity He is giving you. But how are we going to get you ready?"

John Allen rushed to the library with all the Rumania books. He returned home with all the material he could find on Yugoslavia. After packing and saying good-bye to friends each day, he would settle down for an evening of reading about his new homeland.

In late July, 1938, John Allen loaded his suitcases into the back of his sister's car. He said good-bye to his parents and to Reverend and Mrs. Silas Cooper and their two children. Reverend Cooper, pastor of the Tupelo church, had brought his family to say good-bye and wish John Allen well in his new work.

Tears appeared in almost every eye, except Mrs. Moore's. "I have prayed for you all your life," she told her son. "I prayed that God would use you in His service. Now my prayers are being answered. I will not be sad. It will hurt some to think of you being so far away."

"That's natural for us all, Mother," John Allen assured his mother, with a pat on the shoulder. "God is leading. He will continue to lead all of us, step by step. Don't worry. I'll write often."

Working and Waiting

John Allen was not the only student with money worries. Back in Macon, Georgia, Pauline Willingham was trying to figure how she could go to college. Her family did not have money for dormitory rent and dining hall meals. As she thought about the decision, she looked up at her mother one morning. "I've decided I'm lucky," she exclaimed.

"Why, Dear?" her mother asked.

"Because I don't have to go away from home and leave all of you to go to college. We have a college right here in Macon." So, Pauline decided to go to Wesleyan College.

After Pauline had been in school a few months, her mother stopped her just before she went out the door for the third time that day. "I thought you said you were going to *stay home* and go to school."

"Why I am, Mother. It's wonderful. I am enjoying it so much."

"But you are never home. If you are not at school, you are rushing over to the church."

"That's true, I guess. It's just that there are so many things to do at the church. We have such a good group of young people over there."

Pauline graduated from Wesleyan College.

Some days later, after beginning working, Pauline met some old friends. "Have you heard about the trip?" one of them asked.

"What trip?"

"Some young people are going to North Carolina. College students and recent graduates from all over the country will be at a camp there. It's called Ridgecrest. How about going?"

Pauline thought about going to Ridgecrest. It sounded really exciting. Her parents thought so, too. So Pauline made her decision to go.

Ridgecrest proved to be everything she expected. She shared her exciting experience with new friends from all over the country. She attended several meetings. Each taught her something new about how God wanted her to live her life.

One night everyone gathered around a campfire by Lake Dew at the retreat. They were singing the hymn "I'll Go Where You Want Me to Go." Suddenly Pauline quit singing. She bowed her head. "Lord," she said. "I *will* go wherever You want me to go and do whatever You want me to do."

Back at home, Pauline hurried into the house. "Mother," she called. "Ridgecrest was so great. I had such a good time. And, Mother, I told God I would do whatever He wants me to."

"That's wonderful, dear. What do you think God wants you to do?"

"I am not really sure. I guess I need to go somewhere to learn more about what God wants me to do."

"Sounds like you are talking about the Woman's Missionary Union Training School in Louisville."

Pauline and her mother spent the next weeks planning how Pauline could go to Louisville. Finally, the day came. She got on the train and rode to Louisville. They located the school on the corner of Preston and Broadway. Her first look at the school amazed her. It was really very pretty. The trees were in fall colors everywhere. Not very far away was The Southern Baptist Theological Seminary. She stepped on to the Training School grounds, realizing that new experiences awaited her.

Later, some seminary students came over to visit the young ladies. One of these was John Allen. Soon Pauline and John Allen became good friends. Quite frequently John Allen found reasons to see Pauline.

All too soon, Pauline finished her study. She returned to Georgia. First Baptist Church in Tifton, Georgia, asked her to work as secretary and education director. Pauline decided that was what God wanted her to do. She had done what she had promised Him at Ridgecrest.

After work one day, she returned home to find a letter with a strange stamp. She could not read the words on the stamp. She sat down at her desk and tore the letter open. She read it. Then she read it again. She could not believe her eyes. John Allen had written her. He was in Yugoslavia. He had become a missionary. He was learning the language. He was also visiting the churches, conducting conventions, and laying the groundwork for the seminary in Yugoslavia.

Getting the letter was quite a surprise. John Allen wrote Pauline many things about his work in Yugoslavia. Then John Allen asked Pauline to come to Yugoslavia and marry him!

Pauline read the letter over again. Then she put her head in her hands. What a decision! What should she do?

Suddenly her eyes snapped with excitement. She knew what to do. Just what she had done at Ridgecrest. She would ask God. She would do what He wanted her to do.

Still, questions raced through her mind. Yugoslavia was a world away. She had no idea what life would be like there. She was not sure she wanted to get married. She was certainly not sure she should be a missionary. She did know one thing. She wanted to go where God wanted her to go.

John Allen and Pauline wrote many letters to each other. May came. Flowers burst forth in brilliant colors. A friend was graduating in Louisville. She invited Pauline to come for the graduation services. During the worship service, God helped her make the decision.

She went back to her room and picked out the prettiest dress she had brought to Louisville. Slowly, she pulled it over her head. She fixed her hair just so. Then slowly she walked across the street to a flower stand. Carefully she looked over the flowers, unable to decide which to get. Finally, she went up to the man selling the blooms.

"Could you help me find the prettiest flower of all to pin on my shoulder?" she politely requested. "It's for a very special time."

The man quickly chose a beautiful rose. "How's that?"

"Perfect!" Pauline exclaimed enthusiastically as she paid for the rose. With trembling hands, she pinned it on the shoulder of her dress. "Ouch! That hurt!" she exclaimed. "I stuck myself."

Excitedly she almost ran back to the room where she was staying during her visit. She rummaged around in her suitcase for paper. Then she looked through her purse for a pen. She sat down at her table and wrote a few lines. Not satisfied, she wadded the paper up and tossed it into the wastebasket. Again she wrote, frowned, and threw the sheet away. She walked around the room thinking of the many letters they had written since John Allen had asked her to marry him. This was the most special of all. It had to be just right.

Pauline sat down and wrote again. This time Pauline wrote her acceptance of John Allen's proposal. After she wrote her "yes," she felt happier. Pauline felt just right in

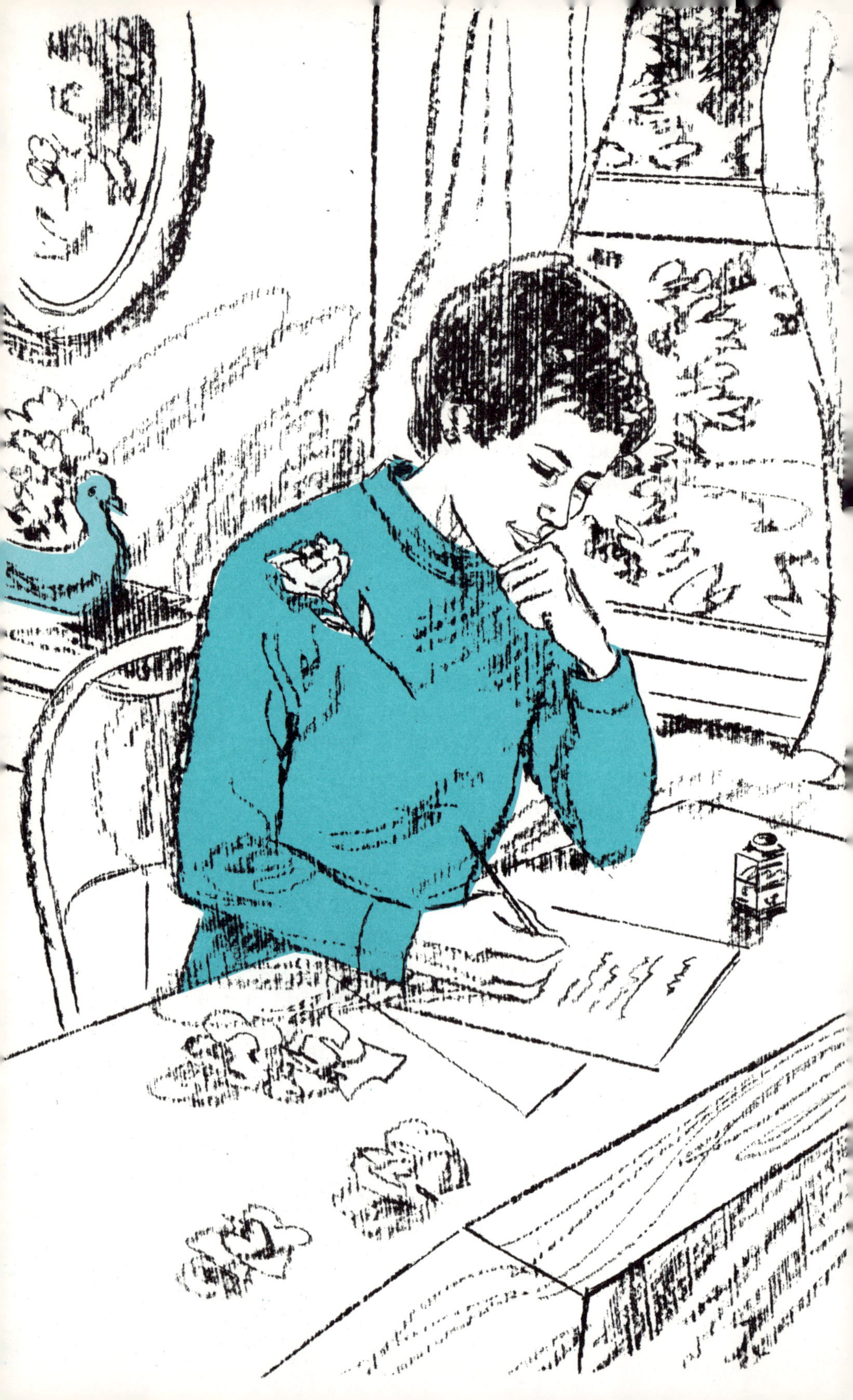

the dress and flower which she had picked out to wear while writing the letter.

Pauline hurried downstairs to mail her answer. She felt good inside. Somehow she knew again she had found what God wanted her to do. She was sure God would help her in the busy days ahead.

Those days proved she needed God's help. Everything was not quite as simple as she had hoped. She had to go through all the tests to become a missionary, too. Finally, she had filled out all the papers and answered all the questions. Then she had to go to Richmond.

"Oh, if Uncle Robert were only here," she thought. Robert Willingham had been the executive secretary of the Foreign Mission Board. He was dead now. Pauline stood before the Board on her own.

"Now Miss Willingham," one member began. "Do you really want to be a missionary? Or do you just want to get married?"

This shocked Pauline into silence. For once in her life she could not think up a good answer. Then she heard a familiar voice. Her first cousin was also a member of the Board. "I am the niece of the late Dr. Robert Willingham. I married a Moore. I think it is a good thing for a Willingham to marry a Moore and serve the Lord." No one else had further questions. Pauline Willingham became a missionary.

She returned home to Georgia and prepared to sail for Europe on September 10. On September 1 she ran down the steps to get the morning newspaper. She opened it at the breakfast table. "Oh, no!" she exclaimed loudly.

"What is wrong, Pauline?" her landlady wanted to know.

"Look at the paper. Germany has invaded Poland. My German ship sailed away last night for Europe. What can I do now?"

"Don't give up yet, Dear. Maybe things will quiet down. You can get another ship."

Things did not get better. They got worse. The United States Department of State wrote Pauline. They had decided to cancel her passport because of the war. She could not leave the United States.

Pauline's spirits plunged. What was wrong? She wanted to do what God wanted. She had tried. What went wrong? She was so confused. Sadly, she sat down at her desk and wrote again. She told John Allen that her passport had been canceled. She told him that she could not come.

"We will have to wait until after the war to get married," she wrote.

The Case of the Chocolate Mashies

In Europe, John Allen was concerned. He did not know where Germany might invade next. He did not know what had happened to Pauline. Had all his plans gone out the window?

Then the letter came. Sadness flooded over him. "Oh, I want her to come. I am so tired of being alone. I am tired of trying to eat my cooking. I am tired of not having someone to talk things over with. Most of all I am tired of not having Pauline with me. Dear God, why can't she come?"

John Allen thought back over the past months. He had tried to learn to live in a foreign country, but it surely wasn't easy. One night he had gone into a restaurant. He wanted a glass of water with his meal. He tried every Serbo-Croatian (SERB-oh-kroh-A-shun) word he knew. None worked. He pointed to his mouth. He put a hand up like he was holding a glass. He pretended to take a big drink of water. He put an imaginary glass on the table. Acting like he had a big pitcher in his hand, he poured water into the glass. He set the pitcher down and took a big gulp of water.

Suddenly the waiter's face lighted up. He turned and rushed into the kitchen. Soon he returned, a big smile on his face and a bottle of the best wine in his hand.

"No! No!" John Allen protested in irritation. He shook his head, put his face in his hands, and cried. "I do not want *wine*. I want *water*."

Five trips with different wines and other drinks finally brought a glass of bottled water to the table. John Allen was glad to pay plenty for the glass of water. As he sipped it, he muttered to himself. "Someday I will conquer this language. I simply refuse to let it get the best of me."

Finally another letter arrived. Dr. J. D. Sadler, the man who directed the Foreign Mission Board's work in Europe, was coming to visit John Allen. "Oh, what will I do for meals," John Allen moaned to himself. Certainly his boss must have the best food possible. Carefully John Allen planned a menu for each meal.

A huge smile brightened John Allen's face as he greeted Dr. Sadler. It was so good to have someone to talk to without having to struggle in a foreign language. He shared his worries and frustrations about Pauline. Couldn't the Board do something to help Pauline come immediately?

John Allen tried to hide his sad, discouraged feelings. Still Dr. Sadler felt John Allen's mood. He, too, wanted to find a way to get the young couple together. He had to be truthful. "Our hands are tied. In these conditions, we can do nothing," he told John Allen.

The clock said it was time for lunch. John Allen's menu called for mashed potatoes. He tried to think back. Just

35

how had his mother fixed them? He began the process as well as he could remember. He put the potatoes in a pan of water and boiled them. He mashed them up. Still, something was wrong. They needed some kind of liquid. But he did not have any milk. Then he saw the hot chocolate he had made for breakfast. He had a little left. Quickly, without a second thought, he poured it in the pot of potatoes.

Then he looked at the finished product. "What do I have here?" he thought. "Why chocolate mashies. That's it! I will call them chocolate mashies." Proudly he took them in and spooned some onto Sadler's plate. The executive looked down at his food.

"Is this a new Yugoslav dish you have learned to fix?" he asked politely.

"Oh no. It's chocolate mashies, a specialty of the house," John Allen replied cheerfully.

"Chocolate what?" his boss asked. Courageously, he lifted a few spoonfuls to his mouth. Soon he found reason to renew the conversation about Pauline and ignore the chocolate mashies.

Later that evening John Allen scraped the rest of the chocolate mashies into the garbage. "Guess we won't try these again," he decided. "The house will have to come up with another specialty."

One December morning, the door bell rang. A young man handed John Allen a cablegram. "What *can* have happened now?" he groaned to himself, as he tore open the envelope. He read the words hurriedly. "What? Can it really be?" He read again more slowly.

"PAULINE SAILING 27th STOP SUGGEST YOU MAKE WEDDING ARRANGEMENTS STOP SADLER"

John Allen threw his hands joyfully into the air. Finally,

his hopes and dreams were coming true. God had not forgotten him. He fell to his knees and prayed, "Oh, Father, thank You for this wonderful news. Forgive me where I have not trusted You enough. Help me be a good husband for Pauline. Amen."

Pauline was happy, too. She had waited so long for this moment. She wanted so much to be with John Allen. She knew he needed her. Dr. Sadler had told the chocolate mashies story to everyone.

With growing excitement Pauline packed her goods. She wanted to be ready in plenty of time. She tucked a few extra goodies in a corner of her luggage. She wanted to surprise John Allen. She had heard Europeans did not like peanut butter. John Allen's sister sent the peanut butter, thinking her brother could buy none in Yugoslavia.

Christmas Day, she knelt with her mother and dad to pray. Mr. Willingham led them.

"Oh, dear Lord, Today is Christmas Day. On the day of Your birth I want to give a gift to You. I want to give You my daughter, Lord, so she can serve You. Amen."

Pauline would never forget those words.

Pauline climbed aboard the train to New York. She determined to leave her family with a cheerful smile. It was hard. Finally she was on the train. She watched the railroad station fade into the distance. Tears began to trickle down her cheeks.

Moments later she turned her thoughts to the adventure which lay before her. She thought about how exciting her life was going to be. How many of her friends in Macon would ever get the chance to travel to New York, much less to sail across the ocean? She had never dreamed of a wedding in Italy!

In New York, she met Ruby Daniel, a missionary to Hungary. Pauline saw Ruby first. As Ruby threw her arms around Pauline's neck, Pauline let out a huge sigh. "Finally," she thought, "I feel safe. It is so good to have a friend who can sail with me."

The two women shared a cabin on the small Italian liner, *Conte di Savoia*. They stowed their baggage and climbed up to the deck. Looking out on New York harbor, Pauline decided, "This is going to be fun."

The crowded ship with many seasick people did not prove to be the best party Pauline had ever attended. The food certainly was not what people in Georgia served their guests! Pauline would never really forget her trip on the *Conte di Savoia*.

Days later the ship finally pulled into dock at Naples, Italy. Pauline stood on deck, hand over her eyes, straining to see the land. Suddenly she tugged at Ruby's elbow. "There he is. See him over there to the right. Isn't he handsome!"

Pauline rushed off the ship as fast as her baggage would let her. She tossed the bags to the ground and threw her arms around John Allen's neck. "It's really true. I'm not dreaming," she exclaimed. "I did not think this moment would ever come."

Quickly John Allen slipped a small package out of his pocket. He took the ring out of its box and slipped it onto Pauline's finger. "Now we are officially engaged," he smiled.

"Oh! It is so beautiful," Pauline said softly. "I had not expected this. Thank you for making me so happy."

"Everything is all set," John Allen told Pauline. "Dr. and Mrs. Dewey Moore, our missionaries here in Italy, have arranged everything. You will have to understand that they do things a little differently here. We will have to have two weddings."

"Two weddings!" Pauline echoed. She stopped to digest the new information. "You are right. They really do things differently here. What do you mean?"

"First we have to have a wedding with a government official. That way the state will recognize that we are married. Then we will have our religious wedding at the Dewey Moores' house. I know you want to have a religious wedding."

Pauline still remembers those adventuresome days in Italy. She had never seen anything like the Italian government officer. He had come to conduct the official state wedding. A red ribbon crossed from his shoulder to his waist, where it was pinned with a bright sunburst.

"Whoever thought you could be at your own wedding and not understand a word that was said?" thought Pauline. She was so glad to have an Italian friend of Dewey Moore's translate every word for her and John Allen. After it was over, the friend assured them they had said the right words at the right times. They were officially married in the eyes of the Italian government.

The religious ceremony was beautiful. But it was not really in a church, like Pauline had dreamed of. It was in the Dewey Moores' Italian home. Dr. Dewey Moore was the preacher for the "church" wedding of John Allen and Pauline Moore.

John looked at his lovely bride. She was wearing a gorgeous lace-covered dress. How could she have gotten that all the way to Europe?

Pauline noted the look in John's eyes. She laughed to herself. She could just hear her mother now. "Pauline, you just do not have room to take that dress. I am thrilled you want to be married in my wedding dress, but you cannot lug it clear across the ocean."

Her mother should have known better. When Pauline was determined to do something, she did it. Pauline's mother would not touch the dress to alter it. Sister Sarah had let out the waist to make it large enough. Then she had carefully sewn the old lace onto net to keep it from tearing. Together they had lugged in a small trunk and put the dress inside. The trunk would hold nothing else. Pauline laughed again as she thought of her mother looking at that one trunk filled only with the wedding gown.

Now on her wedding day, Pauline knew the trouble had been worth the joy of that moment. She shifted her white lilac bouquet to her other hand and grasped John Allen's arm for the ceremony.

Afterwards, she greeted new friends at the small reception. She had quickly learned how missionaries always have a family-like fellowship everywhere they go. She had not only become John's bride, she had become part of that missionary fellowship.

That night in the hotel in Rome, she had thought back over the day. She remembered all the problems they had had. Even the date of the wedding had been engraved on her ring incorrectly. They had planned to be married on January 9. Italian government delays made them wait until the tenth. Inside her ring, the Europeans had carefully written "9-1-40" as the date of her wedding. When she first looked at it, Pauline was puzzled. John Allen explained

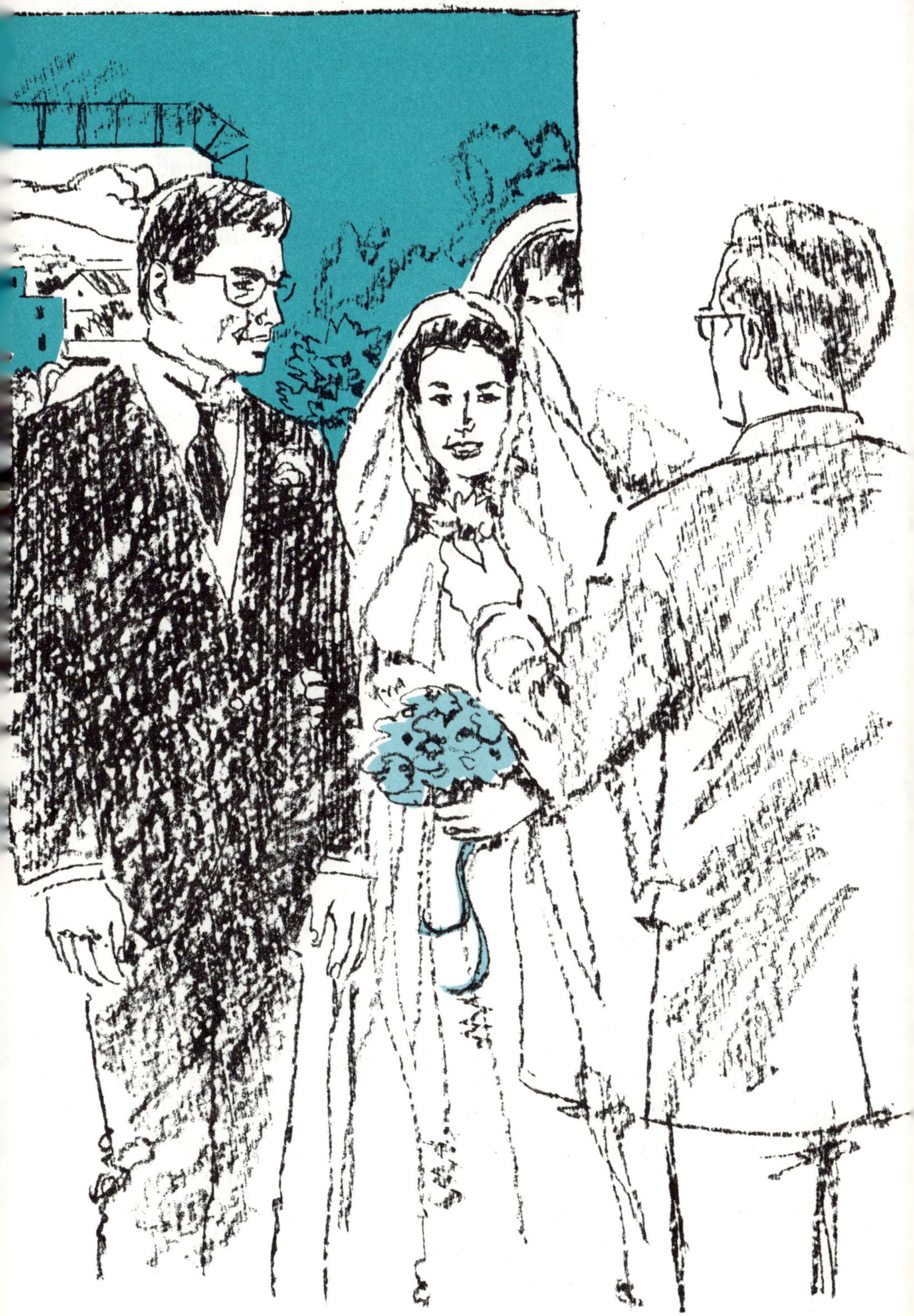

that the Europeans write dates differently from Americans. In Europe the day is always written first, then the month. Those at home who would look in Pauline's ring would probably think she married "September 1" instead of "January 9."

Pauline looked at the lovely little red book the Italians had given her. This was her wedding certificate. It included several blank pages. She and John Allen were to list the names of their children there.

Then she remembered what she had promised, with the help of a translator, during the ceremony. She had pledged to go where John went. If he became ill, she had promised to support the family. Those were not the vows she had expected to say, but she was certainly happy to say them. She was so glad the waiting was finally over. Here she was in Rome as Mrs. John Allen Moore.

War

September had arrived in Belgrade, Yugoslavia. John Allen was so glad he finally had gotten the small seminary started. He was proud of its six students. He and Pauline had agreed on one very practical lesson they wanted the students to learn. They found a large zinc tub. They placed it in the center of the basement of the building which they had obtained for the seminary.

Then they called a meeting of the entire student body. All six students walked down to the basement. They were somewhat puzzled, unsure of what class met in the base-

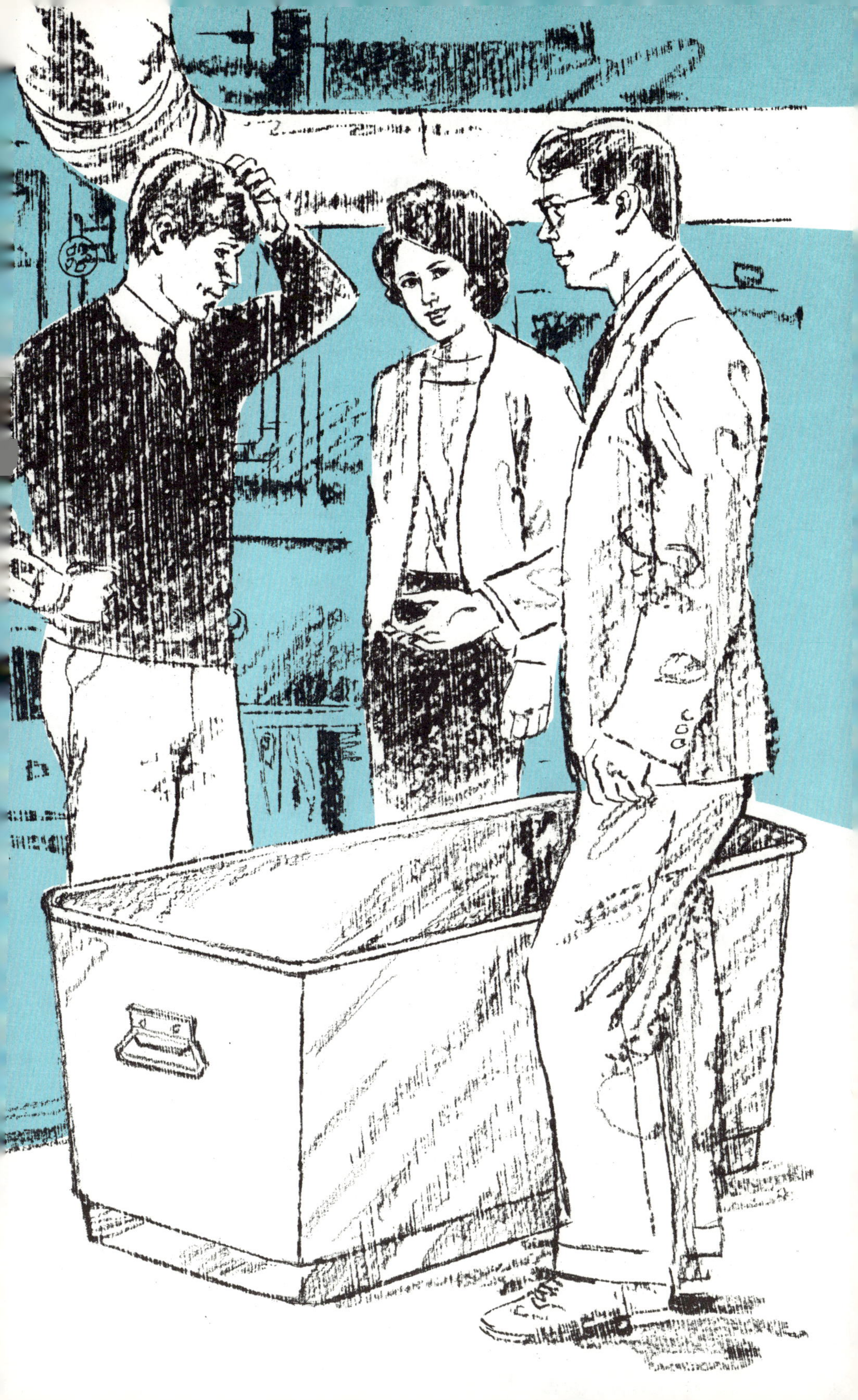

ment. John Allen and Pauline talked about the need to take baths. The students filled the tub with water. John said to one of the students. "After we leave, you may be first," he said. "Tonight is bath night." The student looked around the room. His face was a big question mark. He looked doubtfully at the tub of water.

"Sir, should I take off my clothes first?" he asked.

Trying not to chuckle, John Allen assured the young man he needed to take his clothes off before he stepped into the tub for a bath. Many times since that night, John Allen remembered that he learned a great lesson that night. He had learned something important about being a seminary teacher. A professor had to teach students much more than Bible, church history, and how to preach. He sometimes had to teach them how to do everyday chores.

One week John Allen and Pauline visited a village in the Macedonian area of Yugoslavia. They met a young girl about twelve years old. Her name was Rosika, and she was ready for the fifth grade. The village school only went through the fourth grade. "Would you like for Rosika to go to school?" Pauline asked the parents. "She could return to Belgrade with us and go to school there." Her parents finally agreed that would be best for Rosika. So three people rode back from Macedonia to Belgrade—John Allen, Pauline, and Rosika.

Back at the Moores' house, Pauline took Rosika to her room. While the girl unpacked her few belongings, Pauline tried to talk with her. "Do you have a toothbrush?" she asked in a motherly way. Rosika shook her head. Pauline tried not to act surprised. "John will be glad to take you down to the store to get one," she whispered gently, placing a hand on Rosika's arm.

Rosika shook her head again. Pauline could not understand what she meant. Was she afraid of going to the store with John Allen? Did she want to go back home? What was happening?

Just then John Allen entered the room. As she did, Rosika pulled a nice toothbrush from her belongings. Pauline shook *her* head. She started to say something to the girl. John Allen quietly led his wife out of the room. He could see the puzzled look on her face.

"What is the matter?" he asked. Pauline told the story. "She said she did not have a toothbrush. I said we could go get one. Then she pulled a toothbrush out of her things. What is going on?"

"Exactly what did she say?" John Allen knew how hard it was to communicate in another language.

"I guess she really didn't say anything," Pauline admitted. "She just shook her head."

"Oh," John Allen laughed. "We do have to learn so many things over here, don't we?"

"What do you mean?" Pauline demanded.

"In the section of Yugoslavia Rosika comes from, when you shake your head sideways, you mean yes. When you nod your head up and down, you mean no." The young couple laughed together happily as they realized how much they had to learn.

"At least we can learn together," Pauline told her husband.

Early 1941 was not the best of times in Yugoslavia. Rumors spread everywhere. Hitler and the Germans were coming. When would they have to face the reality of war? John Allen and Pauline prepared for the worst. They bought as much flour and sugar as they could. They knew soon it would be impossible to buy any at all.

"Where can we store it, John Allen?" Pauline asked.

"What about putting it under the floor in the baptistry of the church? You know we set the pulpit up over the baptistry. We only move it away when we are ready to baptize. Most people would not look under the pulpit for flour and sugar."

45

The Moores celebrated Rosika's birthday. She was born on Valentine's Day, so they combined a valentine party and birthday party. Then they sent Rosika back to her village because of the rumors of war.

Crashing bombs awakened John Allen and Pauline on April 6, 1941, Easter morning. German airplanes filled the skies over Belgrade. John Allen and Pauline gathered the students together for an early breakfast and prayers.

"Get some food together, and let's go," John Allen told the group. Pauline led the way to the pantry. They took a ham and two large loaves of bread. Together they rushed out of the house, down the street, and out of Belgrade. Other refugees joined the seminary group as they started south on foot.

Miles down the road their feet began to ache. Blisters formed. They had no time to worry about that. Belgrade was a major target for the German bombers. They had to get as far away from the city as possible.

From time to time, one of the group shouted a warning. Everyone dived for the ditches beside the road. They heard the roar of approaching planes. Bullets whizzed all around them. They walked most of the way. Occasionally John Allen found a farmer with a wagon and offered to pay for a ride as far as the farmer was going. Sometimes the farmers let them ride a little way.

A train came chugging along. Suddenly it slowed down. People were in and all over it. Using their last bit of energy, the seminary group ran to catch the train. John Allen pushed Pauline into a train car which was already overflowing with people. He planted his own feet firmly on the step, already crowded with other feet. He held on for dear life. The students had to climb on top of the train cars to find places. "Everyone in all of Yugoslavia is trying to escape to the center of the country," John Allen decided as he looked at the mob on the train.

That night the seminary group slept on the kitchen floor in a farmer's cabin. The next night they slept on the floor of a public eating and drinking place in a small village.

Finally they reached the mountain village of Pecka. (PETS-kah) John Allen hoped he could continue the seminary classes there. He thought maybe the war would go on only in the cities and valleys below. John Allen looked for a place to stay. No one wanted to take in strangers. The Pecka people thought John Allen, Pauline, and the seminary students were German spies.

Finally, an old man named Alexander had the courage to say, "You can stay in the cabin behind my house." He led the group down the unpaved street to his house and the cabin.

"You must not leave this place," he warned. "Mean men could do you harm. My grandson will run errands and get food for you."

The students joined John Allen and Pauline in prayer that night.

"Dear Father," John Allen prayed. "We do not understand why people have to fight wars. We know they need the Prince of peace. Please accept our thanks that You have brought us to this place safely. Thank You for our new friend Alexander, who has given us this place to sleep. Amen."

Pauline and the students echoed his "Amen."

Two days later they heard Germany and other armies had overrun the country. Pauline and John Allen decided they must get back to Belgrade. "At least we are known there," John Allen said. "But the Germans have their army between us and Belgrade. We can only make it if we sneak in somehow."

They walked down the steep mountain road. In a village at the bottom, John Allen found a Serbian farmer. He agreed to take them to Valjevo in his wagon. They climbed in and rattled down the road.

Just outside Valjevo they found a German patrol. It was nearly midnight. The Moores slouched in the back of the wagon, not wanting to show their faces. The Serbian farmer and one of the students did the talking. Finally, the German soliders waved them through.

In Belgrade again, the Moores heard more bad news. The German commander in the city had issued an order. All foreigners must leave the country. The Moores looked around the city they had grown to love. Sadness filled their hearts. Lovely buildings lay in ruins. German bombs had done their ugly work. German soldiers and Yugoslavs who decided to work with them were everywhere.

One day Pauline looked out the window. "Look," she called. Coming down the sidewalk were three officials or soldiers in their important looking uniforms. John Allen and Pauline watched the soldiers walk stiffly up to their front door. Two Germans stood there. A Yugoslav soldier was with them to translate.

Cautiously John Allen opened the door. "Can I help you?" he asked quietly.

"Did you place this advertisement in the paper offering household goods for sale?" the Yugoslav asked.

"Yes, we did," John answered. He and other foreigners knew they could not take much with them when they had to leave the country. John Allen and Pauline had decided to try to sell as much as possible. John Allen was sure these men did not want to buy the goods. What *did* they want?

The two German officers said something to the Yugoslav. He turned to John Allen. "Jews are not allowed to sell anything."

"But we are not Jews," John Allen explained.

"Prove it!" the Yugoslav demanded, after talking with the Germans.

"Just a minute." John Allen went in and found a box of official papers he had. He chose an insurance policy with an embossed gold seal and colorful lettering. He handed this to the men at the door, hoping they could not read English. Each of the Germans and then the Yugoslav inspected the document carefully.

"In Ordnung!" proclaimed one of the Germans. The Yugoslav translated, "U redu!" This meant "in order" or "all right." The Yugoslav handed the insurance policy back to John Allen. The three soldiers turned and walked away.

John Allen carefully closed the door behind the officers and turned to Pauline with a grin. "This is one time a life insurance policy saved our lives!" he laughed as he put the policy back in the box.

American officials in Yugoslavia could not get their people out immediately. The Moores had to wait a month for the officials to arrange for a boat to take Americans out of the country. The boat, which finally came, made its way up the Danube River to Budapest, Hungary.

Thus, in the middle of May 1941, the Moores were in

Hungary. And John Allen Moore found a new opportunity to teach. Hungarian Baptists had a training school for girls connected with their seminary. "It is a whole lot like our two schools in Louisville," Pauline told John Allen. The Hungarian Baptists asked John Allen to teach in the girls' school.

Hungary proved to be a place of reunion. Some of the Moores' Yugoslav friends had escaped their country and began to study at the Hungarian seminary. Among these was Franjo Klem. He later became an important leader for Yugoslav Baptists. First he was a pastor, then the general secretary in charge of all the work of Yugoslav Baptists. Later he became president of the Yugoslav seminary when it opened again after the war. Franjo Klem was only one of the many young European leaders who got their early training in the ministry from John Allen and Pauline Moore.

The Moores thought they might spend the whole war in Hungary. One day news came from the Foreign Mission Board. "Come quick," John Allen called to Pauline. "We must get what we can in three suitcases and leave immediately. We are going to take a train all the way across Europe to Portugal. Hungary has declared war on the United States, so we must get out of Hungary."

Once more the Moores were on the move. They boarded a sealed train, along with United States government officials and a few other Americans. They were all leaving Hungary. They could not leave the train for a single moment during the earlier days of the trip. Guards stood at each door of the train to make sure no one left.

Finally, they got as far as Spain. "Oh, John Allen. We are in Spain at last. They are going to let us out to stretch our legs. Even a few minutes will make me think I am in heaven."

The few minutes of heaven were soon past. Even when they reached Portugal, the journey was not over. They began immediately to search for a way to get to America. John learned about a small ship, the *Serpa Pinto*. It was sailing for America filled with Jewish refugees. The Jews were fleeing from persecution in Europe. Somehow John Allen managed to get passage on the boat.

After a few days of travel, the Moores began to wonder if they had been fortunate to get places on the *Serpa Pinto*. Two thousand people were on the little ship built to take five hundred. Finally they docked in Cuba. The ship was going on to New York, but the Moores had had enough. They got off at Havana, Cuba.

They found a small Baptist church. A young Cuban man greeted them. "You must come to our youth service tonight," he said. They did go. As the program unfolded, the Moores got quite a surprise. The program was about missionaries. The main story was about John Allen and Pauline Moore, missionaries in Europe!

Eventually they found a ship sailing for Miami, Florida. From there they took a train to Macon, Georgia. "Look, honey. I still have fifty cents," John laughed as they arrived in Pauline's hometown.

Beginning Again

"John Allen! Guess where we are going!" Pauline cried out with enthusiasm. She waved a letter in her hand. "Dr. Sadler wants us to go to Egypt."

"That's great!" John Allen said. "That will be a challenge! God is surely leading. Look at the timing. I have just finished my studies in Louisville. My thesis is written. The work for my doctor's degree is over. I am ready to go to work again. But what can we do in Egypt?"

"We are going to help refugees from Greece and Yugoslavia," Pauline answered. "But, look at this. We are going to have to take separate ships."

"All is well that ends well," John Allen replied with a twinkle in his eye. "The first time you went out as a missionary, I met you in Italy. This time I will be waiting for you in Egypt."

In Egypt the most-needed work proved to be in the Yugoslav refugee camp out in the hot desert. The Moores' call to serve God had carried them to tents in the Egyptian desert. "We almost look like the Israelites led by Moses wandering in the wilderness," Pauline decided one day.

As they rested from their work one day, they looked up to see ships in the distance. "They are sailing through the Suez Canal," John remarked.

"They look beautiful," responded Pauline. "It almost looks like the ships are sailing in the sand."

"They would be beautiful," John Allen agreed, "except for one thing. They are carrying things to make war with. War is always ugly."

John Allen and Pauline were welfare officers in the camp. He often passed out clothing to the poor people. Pauline worked with the children. She could not speak to them much in their language, but she could play games with them. She loved them and tried to show them how much God loved them.

In the summer of 1945, good news came again. The war with Germany was over. The Moores again set sail from Egypt for the United States. This time they were on a ship with American army troops from the European area. It was like a victory celebration.

On the way home another celebration broke out. The captain of the ship announced more good news. The war with Japan was over, too. Everyone could go home and enjoy peace.

John Allen began teaching at Baylor University. One day, the screen door banged shut. John Allen eased his tall frame into their little house in Waco, Texas. He had finished another day's teaching. He sat down in his favorite chair and mopped the sweat from his forehead. "Boy, it's been hot today." Then he added, "Are you ready to move again, Pauline?"

"Here, have a glass of lemonade, John Allen. What in the world are you talking about?"

John Allen gulped the drink down gratefully. The one-hundred-degree weather was almost too much for him. "I'm talking about going back to Europe."

"Well, we've been talking about that for quite a while now. What's new?"

"Just a phone call from Dr. Sadler today."

"Well, why didn't you say so? What did Dr. Sadler have to say? Are we really going back to Europe?"

"Sit down and let's talk about it for a minute."

Pauline sat down and looked straight at her husband. "OK, I'm sitting down. Let's have it."

"What would you think of our working for the Lord in Switzerland?"

"Switzerland? What would we do there? I don't think the Foreign Mission Board has any work in Switzerland."

"Well, it will have. We will be working with European Baptists to start a new seminary."

"A new seminary? Where will it be?"

"Well," said John Allen, slowly. "It looks like it might be in Ruschlikon, a little village down the lake from Zurich. They plan to have students from all over Europe and perhaps from many other countries, too. Since Switzerland is not tied to the East or to the West politically, Dr. Sadler thinks we can get students from countries in the East, too. We ought to be able to see many of our friends from Yugoslavia and Hungary. They want me to teach church history and missions."

In the next few days, Pauline and John Allen scurried around excitedly. They had a lot of packing to do. They also had to get their passports, medical records, and other papers up to date. Finally everything was ready. They boarded the ship in New York. This trip was much more pleasant than their fearful journeys across the Atlantic during wartime. Soon they were on a train in Switzerland, excitedly watching for the Zurich station.

For a while, John Allen and Pauline and two other couples lived in a small hotel. The six of them were to work together to start the new seminary. Even before the land in Ruschlikon was officially bought, they went out to see it. John and Winkie Watts took the Moores out in their little car. Pauline blinked her eyes as she stared at the beautiful mansion. It had a tile roof with chimneys and spires rising above it. Outside the building stood tall trees, lovely flower gardens, and hedges. Two long narrow fish ponds ran down the sides of what would later be the seminary campus. Beautiful ivy covered some of the walls of the fine big house.

"Oh, John Allen! It is so beautiful!" Pauline exclaimed as they walked through the main building. "People who come here to study will be so fortunate. I hope we can make it into a seminary that will bless young people. We want to help them do their best for God."

Pauline walked outside again. "John Allen," she called out. "Have you seen this?" John Allen joined her and gazed out at the blue, blue Lake Zurich. Then he looked farther down the lake and saw the snow-covered mountains reflecting in the gleaming sun.

Pauline and John began to work at the seminary. The first order of business was to get furniture and workers. Women

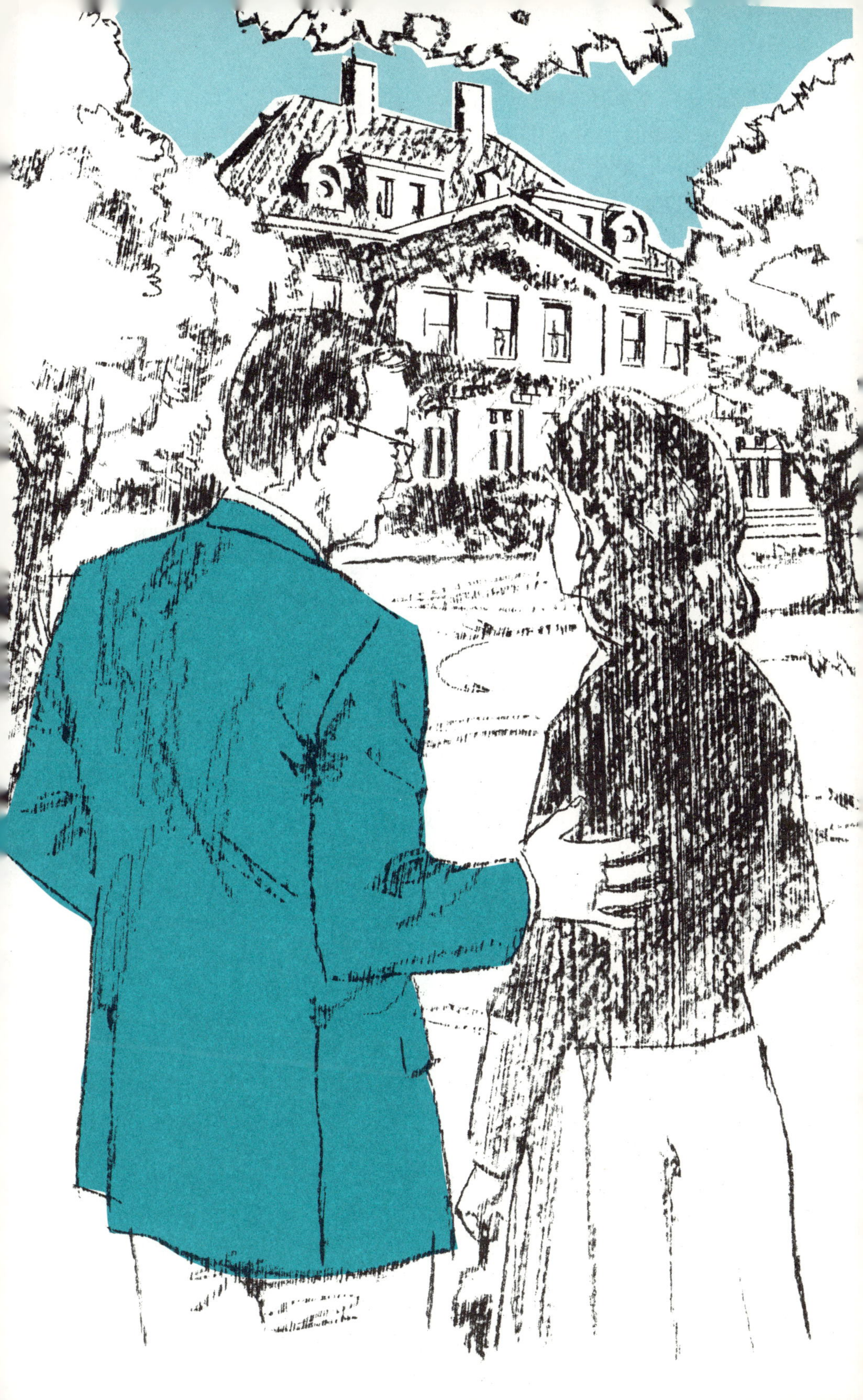

from nearby Baptist churches agreed to serve as housekeepers and cooks. They helped select household supplies.

Pauline and Winkie looked around the largest room. They had decided it would become the chapel. Bright tapestries featuring long-necked birds covered the walls. "Their feathers are beautiful," laughed Pauline, "but they do not exactly lead me to worship."

In later years the tapestries were taken away. The walls were painted with a pretty color.

After a year of hard work, everything was ready. Students began to move into their rooms on the third floor. The students brought vivid memories of World War II with them. They were studying to become preachers.

One day, one of the wives from Holland had begun talking to a German student as they stood on the upper terrace. They admired the roses below. They looked out at the beautiful lake stretching into the distance.

"I still remember the trains that picked up children, mainly Jews, and took them out of our country," she had said. "We never knew what happened to those poor children packed into the German trains. It was just awful!"

The German boy had shrugged. "What is to be will be."

Pauline likes to tell the next part of the story. "Do you know what that young lady did?" she asks. "She was so mad she gave this German a big shove. He fell right off the upper terrace and landed smack in the center of the rose bushes below. That was part of our seminary's growing pains," Pauline laughs. These seminary experiences can be laughed at now. At the time they were very painful.

John Allen enjoyed having students from England, France, Italy, the Netherlands, Norway, Sweden, Denmark, Germany, Yugoslavia, and even Africa. "It certainly enriched our study of church history," he says. "The students gained new self-confidence from seeing how important Baptists have been in Christian history."

John Allen and Pauline had wanted but did not have

children of their own. In May 1951, they started out by train for Austria for a vacation. They rode through Germany and decided to stop at some child placement offices. They asked the Germans about their adopting children. The Swiss did not let foreigners adopt their orphan children. Pauline and John Allen could not adopt children in Switzerland.

They stopped in Hanover, Germany. They went to the government office where a nice woman said she would help them find a child. She took them to different children's homes. Two children's homes had a child the Moores could adopt. Both of the children had been born on August 3, 1950. They were nine months old.

At breakfast the next morning, John Allen looked at Pauline. "This is a big day for us, isn't it? Which do you want, the boy or the girl?"

"I want both of them! I have always wanted twins. This way we have 'twins.'"

When everything was arranged at the government office, the lady took them to the two children's homes. The Moores got both babies. At midnight they wrapped them up and carried them into their third-class train-car for the ride back to Switzerland. They had to lay the babies wrapped in their blankets on wooden railroad benches. It was a long train ride back to Switzerland with their infant twins!

At the border, John Allen had problems. They had to change trains. Pauline got the babies on board the new train, but John could not find which car they were in. Just as the train started to pull out, John Allen saw Pauline looking through the window. Running, he jumped up the steps and into the train.

They wrapped the babies up carefully as the train moved into Ruschlikon station. They saw a Swiss friend there. He helped them take the babies and baggage up the hill to their home.

The new Moore babies surprised the seminary community. "What in the world have we here?" a friend asked.

"The newest Ruschlikon students," John Allen replied with a smile. "We can add two more Germans to our list."

Looking back now, Pauline notes, "We never did get to Austria for that vacation."

Lady Preacher

"My visa for Yugoslavia has come!" Pauline cried as she ran into the living room. "My visa to Yugoslavia came today."

"What about mine?" John Allen asked.

"You didn't get one, I'm afraid," said Pauline.

The Moores had wanted to return to Yugoslavia for a long time. Their hearts had never left the Yugoslav people. Finally they had decided to leave the seminary in Switzerland and move to Vienna, Austria. There they would be closer to the Yugoslav border. From there they hoped to get a visa easier to return to Yugoslavia. They felt strongly that they needed to minister again in Yugoslavia.

Now Pauline had her visa, but none had come for John Allen. What should they do? Finally, John Allen said, "You will just have to go by yourself. The churches need our ministry. If I cannot go, you must go before your new visa runs out."

"But what can I do?" asked Pauline. "You are the preacher."

"God provided you the visa. He will show you what to do and how to do it," John Allen assured her.

So Pauline left John Allen and the twins in Austria. The

twins were in school part of the day. An Austrian woman came to cook and clean and care for the twins when they were not in school.

For a month Pauline visited many of the churches in Yugoslavia. She will never forget the experiences in one country church. Men sat quietly on the right side. Women sat quietly on the left side. They sang a hymn. The men had a long period of prayer. They sang another hymn. The women had a long period of prayer. Then the pastor introduced Pauline as the speaker.

"What can I as a woman do here?" she thought. "It is clear they have separated the men from the women. They must have strong ideas about what men should do and what women should do. Do they really want a woman speaking to the men? I know, I will just face the women and talk to them. I can't help it if the men hear, too."

John Allen was anxiously awaiting to hear all the reports when Pauline returned. She told him all the exciting news. She reported about the many friends he had and how each was serving God. But she also had to report the bad news. "It looks like we will never be able to live in Yugoslavia again. The government will not permit it."

John Allen took that news rather hard. "Why did we ever move to Vienna then?" he asked. "We prayed about it. We were sure we were doing what God wanted. But now we are here with nothing to do. We cannot wait forever to get back into Yugoslavia."

"God knows what is best for us, I am sure," Pauline tried to reassure John Allen.

"I know," John Allen said. "Let us thank God for the good trip you had to Yugoslavia. We will ask Him to show us what He wants us to do here in Vienna."

The answer came much sooner than the Moores had expected. Revolt broke out in Hungary. Thousands of Hungarians began to leave the country to save their lives. They rushed across the border to Vienna, Austria. There they needed help—food, clothing, a bed to sleep in, a chance to plan for their future, a friend.

Money that Southern Baptists gave to the Foreign Mission Board made it possible for John Allen and Pauline Moore to be the friends the Hungarian refugees needed. They let eight of those who escaped live in their house for a while. John Allen set up a camp to care for the refugees. Pauline helped find ways for the people to go to new countries where they could start life over again. The Moores quickly knew that moving to Vienna had not been a mistake. It gave them one of the best years of their lives.

When the Moores moved back to Ruschlikon, John Allen found out something else about how God works. "I studied journalism and enjoyed writing as a young man," he often thought. "It would be nice to be able to use that journalism study in my work."

In Ruschlikon he found European Baptists had a new job for him. They wanted news of European Baptists to be sent around the world. They needed a person to attend Baptist meetings and report on what the churches were doing. They decided to set up the European Baptist Press Service. They asked John Allen to take charge of it.

He gladly accepted the assignment. It proved to give him as much joy and happiness as any work he ever did. His reports showed the small European Baptist churches that the work they did was important. God helped him in his work. Baptists around the world were interested.

Later, the Foreign Mission Board chose John Allen for another assignment. They named him field representative for all the Southern Baptist missionaries and countries in Western Europe. He traveled to all the places where Baptist missionaries were serving. He tried to be a pastor to them. He helped them try to solve any problems they had. He also served as a link between them and the United States.

He tried to find out what the missionaries in Europe needed. Then he talked with people at the Foreign Mission Board in Richmond. He helped determine how many of the needs in Europe could be met with the people and money available. Missionaries all over Europe appreciated his helping them in times of trouble. Together they all worked hard for God.

John Allen also represented the Foreign Mission Board in the communist countries of Eastern Europe. Missionaries could not live in these countries. John Allen could visit the churches and Baptist leaders there regularly. The Foreign Mission Board gave money to help these church members build buildings and do their work.

Finally the day came, in 1978, when John Allen and Pauline moved back to the United States. They moved to Brownwood, Texas. Although they retired from overseas mission work, they certainly have not retired from God's service. They simply moved to a new location.

Pauline became mission study chairman for the Baptist women's organization in her church. She also became chairperson for the church's prayer committee. She has the church members praying for missionaries around the world.

Pauline became director of the Senior Adult Sunday School department. She and John Allen visit many of the church people who are lonely and sick. They also help young children in the area who need to learn to read better. Most of these children are from poor families. They have not had the chance to learn as most children have.

John Allen continued to use his writing skills. He writes books, articles, and news stories. He became the reporter for a retired persons group and submits news of their activities to radio stations, newspapers, and television stations.

The boy from Tupelo, Mississippi, and the girl from Macon, Georgia, have traveled a long way together serving

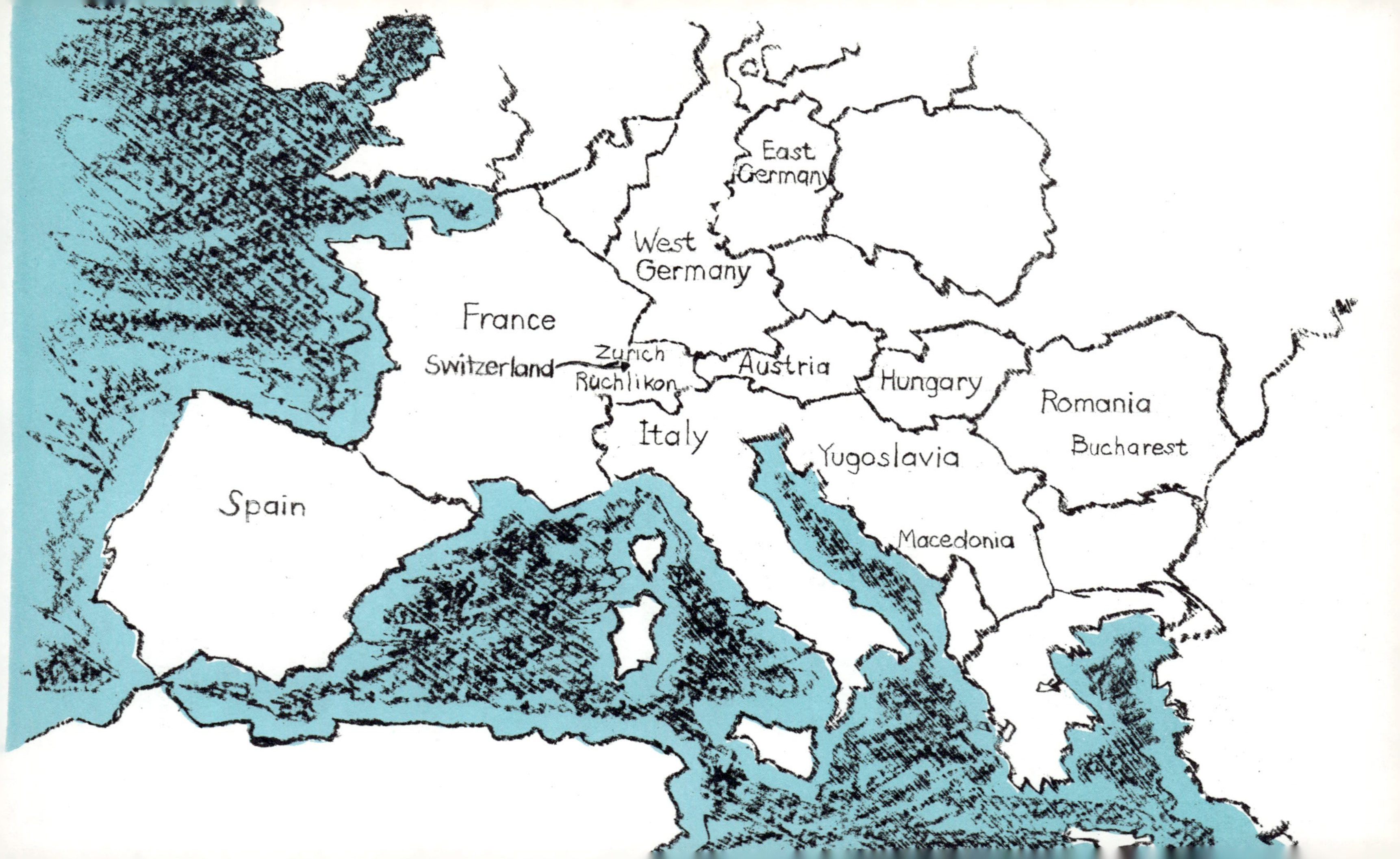
East
Germany
West
Germany
France
Switzerland
Zurich
Rüchlikon
Austria
Hungary
Romania
Bucharest
Italy
Yugoslavia
Macedonia
Spain

their Lord. Their world travels have slowed down now, but they continue to go. Wherever God leads them, they find ways to tell other people how much God loves them and how much He has done for them.

FIRST BAPTIST CHURCH LIBRARY
TOMBALL, TEXAS

Make Your Own Missionary Adventure

- You want to go to college. Your family does not have enough money to pay for college. What do you do?

Where did John Allen Moore get money to pay for some of his college expenses?

- You feel God is speaking to you. He wants you to do some special work. How do you find out what He wants you to do? Does He speak out loud or in some other way?

How did John Allen hear the call of God to serve somewhere as a missionary?

How did Pauline receive her call to serve where God wanted her?

- You want to get married. The person you are going to marry lives in another country. Will you leave your country?

What did Pauline do?

- You know war is going to come to your country. You must store away supplies so you and your friends will have food. What would you do?

What did the Moores do?

- What would you do if you were caught in a war? Would you be afraid? Who would help you with this fear?

What did John Allen and Pauline do?

- What if you had to start a new seminary in a foreign country? What would you do?

What did the Moores do?

- You are still in school. You want to serve God now. What can you do for God today? Write your answer on a sheet of paper.

If God is speaking to you, you can answer Him anytime. You can begin your own missionary adventure right now. Write the following promise on your paper. Then sign your name and write the date.

I will ask God to lead me. I will follow Him wherever He leads.

Meet the Authors

Mary and Trent Butler served with the Foreign Mission Board for ten years from 1971 to 1981. Trent taught in the Baptist Theological Seminary in Ruschlikon, Switzerland. Mary worked in the church. She began a children's Sunday School class with her own two boys and two neighbors in her basement. It grew to include more than fifty children from over twenty-five countries. Mary and Trent also conducted the first Vacation Bible School in Switzerland.

Now Mary and Trent and their sons, Curt and Kevin, live in the United States. Mary is a travel agent and leads tours. Trent works at the Baptist Sunday School Board in Nashville, Tennessee.

Their move to the United States brought some changes to their lives. But one thing did not change. They still work to help people know God.